CHIEF
EXECUTIVE
ATHLETE

CHIEF EXECUTIVE ATHLETE

How to Run Your Sports Career
Like a Fortune 500 Company

SHANNON A. HOLMES, ESQ

publish
y ur gift

CHIEF EXECUTIVE ATHLETE

Copyright © 2022 Shannon A. Holmes

All rights reserved.

Published by Publish Your Gift

An imprint of Purposely Created Publishing Group, LLC

Printed in the United States of America

ISBN: 978-1-64484-498-4 (print)
ISBN: 978-1-64484-499-1 (ebook)

Special discounts are available on bulk quantity purchases by book clubs, associations and special interest groups. For details email: shannon@shannonaholmes.com or call (888) 949-6228.
For information log on to www.PublishYourGift.com

Table of Contents

Foreword

I am absolutely humbled and honored to provide the foreword for this necessary book, *Chief Executive Athlete*.

As the former thirteenth pick in the first round of the 1995 NFL draft, a ten-year NFL veteran, and a two-time Pro Bowl player in the NFL, I must say *Chief Executive Athlete* is a book that is definitely needed in today's sports community. This book will help athletes and coaches navigate the before and after of sports life at the collegiate or professional levels.

Attorney Shannon A. Holmes is the perfect individual to bring this information to light due to his diverse background as an attorney, his experience in financial services, and his experience advising and counseling athletes at various levels. Shannon has a unique ability to understand the athlete and provide guidance that goes beyond the field or court. Shannon has counseled many young individuals, former players, and coaches through the ups and downs of collegiate athletics and the business and sports worlds. I cannot say enough about how excited I am for this book to come forth in today's sports environment.

Congratulations to Attorney Shannon Holmes and his family as he embraces this chapter of his life. Cheers!

Mark Fields

Pac-10 Defensive Player of the Year 1994, former first-round draft pick, ten-year veteran, two-time Pro Bowler, winner of the 2005 Best Comeback Athlete ESPY Award, NFL combine linebacker coach, managing member of MLF Holdings, LLC

Acknowledgments

First, I would like to thank God for his continued blessings and his imparted vision, grace, and mercy! I would like to thank my wife, Dr. Jeane' Simmons Holmes, M.D., for her infinite love and support. When a man finds a wife, he finds a good thing! I indeed found a good thing. I would like to thank my twins, Bryce and Bailee, for the light they shine in my life and their never-ending love, encouragement, and memorable moments. I am thankful to my parents, Bobbie and Anthony "Kee-Zee" Holmes, for being my longest-tenured supporters. Thanks to my brothers, Brian and Todd Holmes, for lending their ears without reservation.

Thanks to Jerry Ball Jr., the first guy from the neighborhood to make it to the National Football League, for teaching me my early lessons in the sports business and your continued trust and support by allowing me to serve as your trusted legal counsel. Thanks to Darrell Colbert Sr. for always including me among your NFL colleagues, being a "big brother," and defining the "Hard Work Pays Off" motto. Thanks to Craig Curry for introducing me to black male professionalism and for asking me the question, "What do you want to do after college?" Thanks to Attorney Carl Poston for taking a chance on me as a young college intern and law clerk and teaching me the sports agency business. Thanks to Sterling Sharpe for your friendship and many words of wisdom regarding the life of an NFL athlete, especially one whose career comes to an abrupt halt. You should know that many of our discussions laid the foundation for this book. Thanks to Mark Fields Sr. for your friendship, trust, and many long conversations about life, business, the plight of the athlete, family, and kids. Thanks to Coach Clarence McKinney and Coach Byron Smith for trusting me as your legal representative. Thanks to Michael Williams (National Basketball Association [NBA]'s record holder for consecutive free throws [97]) for your friendship and trusting your companies with my law firm for legal guidance and counsel. Thanks to my many other clients for allowing me to represent you. Thanks to my law school classmate, section mate, and fraternity brother, Brandon Ball, for his continuous support and serving as a great hype man. Lastly, thanks to my legal assistants, publisher, editor, and marketing team.

Introduction

"If you aren't going all the way, why go at all?"
—Joe Namath, former NFL quarterback

Becoming a professional athlete is a dream come true. Every athlete, at some point in their young lives, has day-dreamed about making a name for themselves on the court or field—signing autographs, gaining endorsements, and improving their lives and the lives of those they love with seven-figure checks. The chances of that dream actualizing? Slim to none! It is estimated that there are more than one million high school football players in the United States. Only about 6.5 percent of them will go on to play in college, and only 1.2 percent of those who go on to play in college will be drafted by the NFL.[1] The odds are even less for basketball. To earn a spot on a professional roster makes you an anomaly. Finding success in life and business when your name is no longer on a professional roster makes you an even bigger anomaly.

This book will teach you—whether you are an athlete, coach, entrepreneur, or entertainer—how to form and treat your personal talent as a business. My goal is to share

---

[1] "Football: Probability of competing beyond high school," NCAA, April 20, 2020, https://www.ncaa.org/about/resources/research/football-probability-competing-beyond-high-school

with you how to treat your athletic talent and coaching skill as a business. I believe there is more to your professional sports career than just saying, "I'm really good at running or catching or throwing, so pay me X amount of dollars, and I'll collect the check and go home." Why short yourself by leaving so much on the table? I want to teach you how to look at your skill as a business in which you provide a service to other businesses.

In a Fortune 500 company, the chief executive officer—or CEO—is the top dog, the highest-ranking person in the company. Our goal is to convert you, the athlete, into the CEO of your team, the one with the last word. However, in this book, you will be referred to as the *Chief Executive Athlete*, or the CEA—different name but same definition. Going forward, you will consider yourself a CEA! There are several parallels between managing a sports career and a Fortune 500 business. The earnings are obviously different, as players are not likely to earn as much as a Fortune 500 company from their talent alone; but in the sense of providing a service, branding your company like a Fortune 500, and having the proper professionals to help you run your business, a sports career and a Fortune 500 company are very similar. Whether you are making the league minimum, or billions as the owner of Amazon, you need to have qualified people in position to help run your organization so that you can accomplish your business and personal goals.

As a professional in sports, you are asked to bear many burdens: performance, personality, lack of privacy, and potential. The following chapters are designed to help protect you from failure due to simply not knowing better—and to guide you in properly positioning yourself to protect your image while taking advantage of the resources that can provide you income and opportunities long after your tenure on the team has ended. While protecting your name, image, and likeness are important, so is the opportunity to earn more than your contract value. In 2021, for instance, the minimum salary in the NFL for the last guy to make the team was $660,000. No college graduate, no master's degree candidate, no PhD or MD is going to make that as a starting salary. Not one! The salary earned by a professional athlete at such a young age is an incredible economic opportunity and serves as an economic and life springboard.

I explain the springboard concept to young athletes all the time. Imagine, if you will, having a really springy diving board as you see at many pools. On that diving board, you have the opportunity to bounce as high as you can and as many times as you want before diving into the water. Similarly, if you perform well by providing your service to the team or organization, leading to increases in your compensation and longer tenure at the highest level in your profession, then you have a chance of *springing* yourself to a higher degree of wealth at a very early age. Performance, tenure, and opportunities inside and outside of your profession (incentives, bonuses, endorsements, and business opportunities) can provide additional income to you. Simply put, you have to position yourself to take full advantage of the opportunities presented to you because of your skills and service. Unless you operate a very successful business or obtain a very lucrative media deal after your playing or coaching career ends, you will likely not have the same opportunities again in life to earn the type of money you earn while playing, coaching, performing, etc.

You know there is a unique opportunity to make big money in your sports career. But you also realize there is more money to be made and you want to pivot and launch into bigger, better things from this space. If this is you, then you are in the right place.

This book will serve as a foundation for you—for anyone who has the desire to be successful outside their sport regardless of background, network, or current knowledge about owning and managing a business, a brand, or an enterprise.

Disclaimer: This book is designed for informational purposes only and not for the purpose of providing legal and/or business advice. You should contact an attorney to obtain advice with respect to any particular legal issue or problem. Use of and access to this book does not create an attorney-client relationship between the author and the reader.

It Starts in College

"I'm not a businessman. I'm a business, man."

—Shawn Carter, rapper, songwriter, and entrepreneur

For some athletes, the business of branding and positioning yourself for profit starts in high school. For most, however, it starts in college. With the National Collegiate Athletic Association's new regulation, which allows college athletes to actually profit from their own names, images, and likenesses, the business is changing. Before we delve into the new regulation, let us revisit life before it.

The National Collegiate Athletic Association (NCAA) is a non-profit organization that regulates student-athletes from more than 1,200 institutions and conferences in the United States and Canada. It was created to protect student-athletes from the physical and financial dangers of the game as well as the business of it. In the 1905 football season, eighteen amateur players died during games. There was talk about abolishing the game of football altogether, so the President of the United States at the time, Theodore Roosevelt, met with thirteen football representatives to discuss safety measures. The NCAA was formed shortly after.

Early on, the NCAA decided that student-athletes should not be allowed to earn money beyond their college scholarships. They felt that free tuition and the opportunity to showcase talent for the professional leagues was sufficient pay. They wanted to keep the amateurs separate from the professionals and considered benefits such as free education, housing, healthcare, and meals as adequeate compensation in exchange for students' participation in sports. Conversely, the university would use sports to generate income for the university. The nerve of them!

The NCAA's next concerns were ethics, clarity, and fairness. Think about Alabama, the University of Southern California (USC), Notre Dame, or any of the really big schools that have an abundant number of financial resources. If you allow them to pay their athletes without any controlling mechanism, those schools will most likely dominate collegiate sports. Smaller schools would struggle to compete. If athletes were paid to attend and compete at the collegiate level, why would a player go to University X for $30,000 a year when he/she could go to University Y for $300,000 a year? So, there was/is clearly a concern regarding inequity among the varying NCAA colleges and universities.

Another concern was the ethics regarding cheating: players being bought! Although sports gambling is now being legalized in multiple states, over the years, there have been many cases where athletes were paid to throw a game or point-shave. What does that look like? Well, there is a three-point spread in a game, in point-shaving, the booster or the gambler pays a kid to not make shots that night, and the team picked to lose by three or more loses by at least three points or more. The gambler bet X amount on the game, won more than he bet, paid the player some, and still took home a lot of money from the return made on the original bet. That game would be considered "thrown" by the player participating in the scheme.

Then there is the opposing argument that student-athletes definitely deserve to be paid. After all, the universities make so much money on the athlete's name, image, likeness, and performance. The arrival of social media has really played a role because athletes are accessible like never before. Before social media, athletes, games, and university images were primarily seen only on TV on Saturdays, and many people did not see those images. But now, when people pick up their phones, whether they are a fan or not or whether one likes sports or not, they still get exposed to sports through social media and various other media. Hence, with the increased exposure for university sports programs and athletes alike, the advocates for paying college athletes are initiating change by challenging the status quo and pushing state legislators and the NCAA officials to reconsider their stance on amateur athletes receiving compensation for their name, image, and likeness. Even megastar LeBron James spoke up on behalf of amateur athletes and challenged the governor of California to change the state laws governing amateur athletics.

Ed O'Bannon, a former University of California, Los Angeles (UCLA) basketball star, sued the NCAA in 2009 in what was considered to be the first serious legal challenge against the NCAA's rules against amateur players being paid. Here is what happened: O'Bannon ended his college career in 1995 when he was drafted by the New Jersey Nets. Almost fifteen years later, after his NBA career had ended, he saw a video game that his friend's son was playing. Ed and his brother Charles, who also played for UCLA, as well as all of O'Bannon's UCLA teammates from 1995, were in the game. O'Bannon realized that however much money the game was profiting, he was not making a penny of it. Not only was he not being paid for it, but he had never given them permission to use his image. Interestingly enough, the use of his image became the crux of the lawsuit and the catalyst for change.

In 2009, O'Bannon sued the NCAA, EA Sports (the video game developer), as well as the Collegiate Licensing Company (who handles university licensing rights). He reached a forty-million-dollar settlement with EA Sports and the Collegiate Licensing Company, but his fight against the NCAA climbed its way to the US Supreme

Court and caught a lot of attention from athletes and non-athletes alike. His argument was simple: My education is done, I am done, we are done, pay me! His case was huge in garnering the necessary attention toward the problem of players not being compensated for their image and likeness while they are in college and even years later. O'Bannon could have shrugged it off, shook his head, and accepted it just the way it is, but he challenged the system, and to a large extent, he won.

Let's look at Zion Williamson. In the 2019 NBA draft, he was the number-one overall pick. Before that, he played for Duke University, averaging 22.6 points and 8.9 rebounds while shooting 68 percent from the field. He is powerful, quick, and explosive. Even in high school, his 360 dunks were already wowing the world. His confidence, along with his collegiate performance to match, led to comparisons between him and LeBron. However, despite his popularity and sheer skill displayed during his one year at Duke University, he was not eligible to be compensated for his name, image, or likeness.

At the start of the 2021–2022 season, college athletes were allowed to be paid for third-party endorsements both related to and separated from athletics. This includes social media and personal appearances. There are a number of other stipulations involved, such as universities not being allowed to pay students for their name and image and, conversely, student-athletes not being able to use the logo or trademark of the NCAA or their university. Most likely, by the time you read this book, college athletes will be earning money from the brands that they worked so hard to create. With that in mind, it is time for players to start really seeing themselves as chief executives—as early as high school, and for some, even sooner.

As a chief executive athlete, you are responsible for your business, which is your name, image, and likeness and the skills you possess, which are packaged up and provided as a service for compensation. Protecting your interest is the key to your success! Two of the primary ways to make sure that you are getting all that you are entitled to are to do your research and employ your team. We will discuss that in depth in Chapter 3. I strongly suggest that your first hire be an attorney who can protect you and your legal interest.

Being offered money can be tricky! Being offered money as an athlete can be even trickier. You could very well make decisions early on in your career that you end up regretting for a very long time. Let's say a local grocery store offers you $10,000 to throw a football to the store owner for a commercial. You sign, book, shoot the commercial, and collect your check. In your contract, however, you granted them sole ownership of your digital image for perpetuity, i.e., forever. Now, no other company can use your image. You just unknowingly signed away your ability to sell, license, and use your own image for other commercial gain.

There is also the concern of whom you attach your name to and for how long. Let us use the same example of the grocery store. The store gets caught up in the middle of a racism or sexism scandal and guess who the media wants to interview about it? You—someone who, most likely, has absolutely nothing to do with it. That association with a twisted set of facts could cost you future endorsements and business opportunities.

Then there are the issues of time and money. You want to be paid sufficiently and you also do not want your name or image tied to a company for too long (without adequate compensation). There is more to the process than just signing your name on a piece of paper. You have to really understand the complete analysis of endorsements, value, contracts, relationships, branding, and so on. A sports attorney and marketing professional can help you through this process.

What if you are the quintessential broke college student, though? How do you afford an attorney when you can hardly afford to keep up with your phone bill? What is fair compensation? Does it have to be hourly? A fixed fee? In most instances, an attorney will work on a contingency basis. This simply means the attorney will be compensated after negotiating your deal and after you receive compensation. Do your due diligence on identifying good and competent legal counsel.

Take your time! I cannot stress that enough. It is better to refuse than to regret. Protect yourself and your image. As Shawn Carter, better known as Jay-Z, pointed out, you are not a businessman, but you are definitely a business! It is time to start branding yourself and protecting yourself as such. Position yourself in this game for not only short-term success—not only to make it into a professional league—but to begin seeing yourself as the business that you are.

You Are the Business and the Brand

"It takes 20 years to build a reputation and 5 minutes to ruin it. If you think about that, you'll do things differently."

—Warren Buffett, CEO of Berkshire Hathaway

A chief executive officer (CEO) is the ultimate decision-maker for a business. As the *Chief Executive Athlete* (CEA), you are the ultimate decision-maker for a business that sells a service. Your service is the athletic performance you provide to a team or organization. Your derivative businesses are the opportunities that result from your performance.

PROVIDE QUALITY SERVICE

Your service is your performance. You are paid to perform. The better you perform, the better you are paid. So, it is imperative to train properly and play well. Seems like that goes without saying, right? It is easy to get distracted, especially when popularity and money come into the picture. As the saying goes, "Poverty is a great motivator."

You will do everything it takes to transcend that status, but once it is attained, it becomes a little harder to go the extra mile. Running thirty sprints seems less appealing when you already have $20 million dollars in the bank. So there has to be another *why*. What is your reason for training hard and committing to your craft? Is it to be the best? Is it the money? Is it the attention? Is it for your family?

There is much criticism these days about players caring more about likes and followers on social media than they do about their bodies and their passion for the game. It is understandable to an extent, considering that huge followings can convert to cash. However, the likes and followers cannot out-prioritize your performance. Consider the fact that the better you prepare and play, the more likes and follows will come—so much so that you will likely need someone else to manage your social media presence for you. Focus on delivering quality service, and the monetary gains will follow. Tom Brady, for instance, won his seventh Super Bowl at forty-three years old. His diet, fitness, and overall preparation is unmatched. The same went for the late Kobe Bryant, who said he would arrive at the gym hours before the rest of the team. "You will not outwork me," he would say. And it showed! Serena Williams is another example of high achievement and hard work. Successful athletes invest a lot of time and money into their ability to play at the highest level.

I am not emphasizing how much money you should spend on training and nutrition but rather how much you should prioritize your craft. You are a business! Your task is to produce the best product. Mercedes-Benz tweaks their cars all the time. Amazon grew exponentially because they continuously tweaked their operations until they became the number-one online retailer. You have to be good at what you do, listen to the feedback and criticisms, and continue to tweak your performance. The likes and follows will come. Underperforming, on the other hand, will neither gain nor sustain the same amount of attention. Also remember that top-level performance can give you an extra year or two. No one wants to get rid of star athletes. Fans, team executives, and corporate partners go to bat for you. On the other hand, subpar players are easily let go.

Your performance is what got you in the door. Staying in the building for as long as possible will be based on your ongoing performance. Your strong performance will help you develop your brand.

BRANDING YOURSELF
For new and emerging CEAs, building a solid personal brand is the first step to establishing a successful business portfolio. After all, your performance and personal brand are the foundation of your business. How you come across to the consumer, the team, the media, and to

potential corporate partners (those companies that may want to pay you to endorse a product) is your brand. How do you appear? What is your image in the public eye? Whether it is a logo or how you sign your name, a picture of you, a number, a color, or a combination of those things, it all ties into your image, your likeness. Your brand is one of your most effective tools for reaching your target market. It determines how your teammates, fans, sponsors, and the entire sports industry will identify you. The best part about it is that you control your brand and can (and should) use it to help enhance your earning opportunities.

A good brand, however, is rarely a result of happenstance. It is strategic. A strong branding strategy can help you form credibility in your market, connect you with your fans, and attract sponsors. It can also help you gain recognition and success that you can monetize for your current and future career plans. You might be wondering why you cannot just bypass the branding and focus on playing. Afterall, that is what got you to this point. I hear you! However, if you desire to have more than the check the team writes you, then you will have to go the extra mile. There is no way around it. Fans want to feel like they know you, and sponsors like Nike, Adidas, and Gatorade want to partner with CEAs who know how to engage their fans on and off the court.

Take, for instance, Deion Sanders. He created "Prime Time," a persona who still sells to this day, twenty years after his retirement from playing. Prime Time is straight-forward, known to "keep it real," fearless in speaking his mind, and downright hilarious. He reminds you of your favorite uncle at the family get-together. Prime Time may not be who Deion is personally, but he is agile enough to turn on that persona when it is required of him to do what he needs to do to earn and create more earning opportunities. It works because it connects him with the people. Deion has enjoyed one of the longest careers as an NFL analyst because of the likeability he cultivated for decades. LeBron James is another example. He has done a great job controlling his brand, image, and likeness in the manner he would like to be perceived. He stood his ground and created his own space, and he leveraged his superb athletic ability to maximize his earnings on and off the basketball court.

Your brand is heavily impacted by your own actions, but the media plays a role as well. As you know, the media will grab something you say or do and use that to build you up or tear you down. That is why you have to really own your space. You have to decide whether or not you agree with what is being said about you and move accordingly. The media might be saying one thing, but if you desire to be known and remembered another way, then you have to create that image for yourself. Essentially, you have to present yourself in the manner you want to be perceived and received. Your words and actions help chart that path.

But again, performance cannot afford to be neglected. In addition to the stellar branding of guys like Deion and LeBron is their undeniable talent and performance. If you pair great performance with a great name, image, brand, likeness, and positive media image, better opportunities are the end result. It is a gold mine! But that does not mean you have to have a contract like LeBron or Stephen Curry to be successful. You just have to play your cards right and fully leverage your opportunities.

Junior Bridgeman, drafted to the NBA in 1975, was not the most notable performer on the court and most likely is not even a recognizable name unless you are a really big basketball fan. He is not nearly as well-known as his contemporaries, Kareem Abdul-Jabbar and Julius "Dr. J" Erving, yet he is one of the wealthiest former athletes in the world. How so? He spent off-seasons studying the Wendy's business model. By the end of his NBA career, he owned three of the fast-food chains. Today, he owns more than 160 Wendy's restaurants, 120 Chili's restaurants, a Coca-Cola bottling company, and more. He leveraged the $350,000 yearly salary he made in the NBA with the opportunities he was presented and catapulted into being a more notable businessman than he was an athlete. So, again, you may not be the highest earner, but that does not mean that your current opportunity will not open doors to other opportunities if you position yourself accordingly.

If you can understand these concepts, look at yourself from a business perspective, and start to identify your goals as a company, you can better understand your needs. You may not need all the exposure some athletes seek because you may want to quietly own commercial real estate, franchises, or some other type of business that does not require your name, image, or likeness to be successful. You may want to create a start-up company or invest in tech start-ups under the guidance of Rashaun Williams of Manhattan Venture Partners. Ultimately, it all comes back to approaching your career from a business mindset, setting goals and objectives, and creating your own dream team (which we will discuss in more detail in Chapter 3).

Your teammates' strategies might not work for you. That is because everyone's paths and goals are vastly different. LeBron was on the cover of *Sports Illustrated* when he was a junior in high school. That is leverage. When he became a professional athlete, his performance matched the media hype. But what about the player whose performance does not match? We all know what happens in those certain instances. The media is going to throw you away. They are going to throw you to the wolves because you are not living up to their expectations. So, there are two key lessons:

1. It is okay to be inspired by other CEAs' brands and career opportunities, but it is important to

individualize your own career aspirations and branding strategies.

2. You cannot live through the media. The media has its own agenda, and as quickly as the media can feel like a friend, they can just as quickly begin to feel like the opposition.

Do you need a multimillion-dollar public relations team? It depends. With the help of public relations (PR) professionals, you will be able to identify what your specific branding goals are for you as a company. Identification of those goals will help you determine what you need, how you should craft your brand, image, and likeness, and whether you need more public relations or more interviews or advertisements. It is all based on your goals, your company's vision. With a team of professionals, you can craft your individual plan and likely get there quicker than you can without a team of qualified professionals. Remember, you are now a company! You need a team of qualified people to help you grow your business.

Building Your Dream Team

"Talent wins games, but teamwork and intelligence win championships."

—Michael Jordan, NBA governor, six-time NBA champion, entrepreneur, philanthropist

You are going to hire a lawyer, an agent, and many other different people along the way to help you in your career. However, unlike a company where all of these hired people are typically in-house, this likely will not be the case for you. Your team will be located in various places, likely even in different cities or states. Your PR team might be in New York. Your agent might be in Florida. Your lawyer may or may not be in the same city as you. While having everyone in a different location is technically a disadvantage compared to having them all in one place, it is not always a bad thing. The team just has to be managed.

Often, you are pitched by individuals and even companies that your career/your company can be managed by one person or one organization. You should certainly carefully evaluate whether that makes sense for you.

Definitely do not try to simplify this process by doing it all on your own or all through one person, *even if it is marketed to you that way.* Do your due diligence! Think like a CEA. You may be approached by an organization or individual who says they are the best marketing company in the United States for athletes and they have a roster to prove it. That is great! You still need to do your research to see if their offerings align with your vision and needs. Your goal should be to build a team that is diverse in terms of expertise, experience, and industry.

In most companies, the company is broken into various departments and each department has leadership and support staff. Can you imagine the salesperson for AT&T attempting to increase the corporate sales of AT&T *and* managing the marketing for the brand or handling accounts payable? That is what it is like when one person—and in some instances, one organization—attempts to manage all the affairs of a sports professional.

You want to approach your business like a Fortune 500 company, preferably one that you admire and would perhaps even like to be partnered with one day. You should take a close look at what that company is doing, how they are structured, and who they have on their team. Nike, for instance, would never have just one person responsible for making their shoes, marketing their shoes, and handling their accounting and contracts. No, they have a chief marketing officer (CMO) who has tons of marketing staff working for them. They also have a "team" of lawyers, a chief financial officer (CFO), and many other competent professionals ensuring their successful operation. You want you and your "company" to mirror what a successful company looks like. This is an intricate piece of transitioning from viewing yourself as an individual to actually considering yourself a business.

One way to mirror your business to that of a Fortune 500 company is to create an organizational chart that visually communicates the company's internal structure by detailing the roles involved, each role's responsibilities, and the relationships between the roles. The purpose of the organizational chart is to represent, in diagram form, who reports to whom; it is the chain of command within the company's dream team. The basic tenets of a team can be summarized by taking a look at Nike's organizational chart.

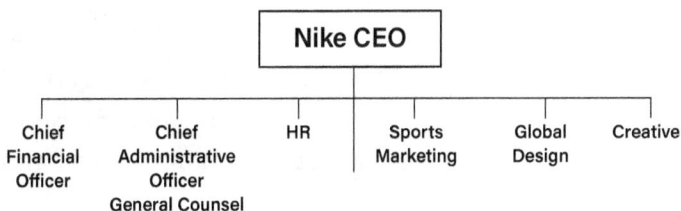

Nike CEO					
Chief Financial Officer	Chief Administrative Officer General Counsel	HR	Sports Marketing	Global Design	Creative

**CHIEF EXECUTIVE ATHLETE
(C.E.A.)**
Organization chart

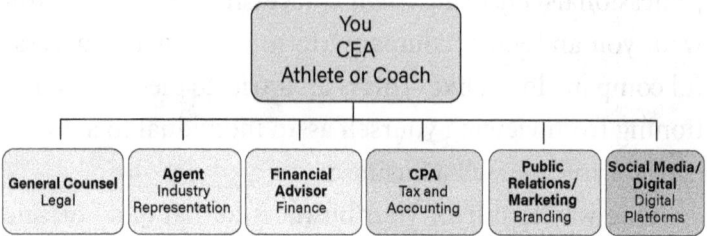

CEA'S ORGANIZATIONAL CHART:

General Counsel: a company's main attorney and primary source of legal advice.

Sports Agent: represents the interest of an athlete or coach, particularly in contract negotiations when negotiating a new contract, contract extensions, or labor disputes.

Financial Advisor (FA) or Certified Financial Planner (CFP): a professional who provides expertise for clients' decisions around money matters, personal finances, and investments; CFP is a formal recognition of expertise (gained through classes and examinations) in the areas of financial planning, taxes, insurance, estate planning, and retirement.

Certified Public Accountant (CPA): an accountant responsible for advising and preparing an organization's tax returns; also capable of representing the organization during an Internal Revenue Service (IRS) audit, hearing, or appeal.

Marketing: a combination of activities that a company employs to influence consumers or other organizations to purchase its products or services.

Public Relations (PR): the professional maintenance or crafting of a desired public image for a company, organization, or individual.

Social Media/Digital Presence: a company or individual that assists an organization in creating a presence via websites, forums, blogs, and social media platforms. A presence in the digital space can enhance your marketability and provide additional business opportunities.

Think about this. The very team/organization/university that you are providing your services to is set up this way. Why would you not do the same thing if you want to have equal or greater success?

A CEO, according to Investopedia, is "the highest-ranking executive in a company, whose primary responsibilities include making major corporate decisions, managing the overall operations and resources of a company, acting as the main point of communication between the board of directors and corporate operations and being the public face of the company."[2] Everyone listed below the CEO on Nike's organizational chart reports to the CEO. John Donahoe, Nike's current CEO, is everyone's boss at the company. He is also the public face of the company.[2]

There are a number of similarities and differences between a CEO and you as a CEA. Both are the top bosses! You are at the top of the chart, meaning everyone answers to you. The operations of the company might be delegated to various persons, but you are primarily responsible. If the ship sinks, no one is looking at the employees. They are looking at you. The same is true for when business is going well. That is because you are the face of the company. What is different, however, is that the CEA has a lot more power. Let me explain!

A CEO is usually appointed, chosen by board members. John Donahoe, before becoming Nike's CEO, was the CEO of eBay. He was appointed CEO of Nike in October of 2019 and started his new role in January of 2020. Although he is the top dog, he still has to answer to the board. The board represents the interest of the shareholders (i.e., the real owners of the company). The board also has the power to fire the CEO and replace him or her.

Part of the definition of chief executive officer is making managerial decisions. The definition of a CEO further breaks down what those managerial decisions are and

---

[2] Adam Hayes, "Chief Executive Officer," Investopedia, November 10, 2021, https://www.investopedia.com/terms/c/ceo.asp/

what management does. Management consists of inter-locking functions: creating policy, organizing, planning, controlling, and directing. Again, those tasks are relegated to you as *Chief Executive Athlete*; that is what you have to provide in terms of direction to your team. Then your team is tasked to come back to you and express their thoughts, discoveries, and suggestions for their respective areas of the company. In essence, it is your team's role to use their expertise to share the pros and cons of the company's next move(s) with you, the CEA. Since you are a privately held company without a "formal" board of directors, you might be asking yourself, how does a board of directors relate to your company and how does the board function?

BOARD OF DIRECTORS

Outside of the internal organizational chart, there exists another center of influence, and that is your board of directors. In large organizations, the board of directors represents the interest of the shareholders and defines the goals that are carried out by the CEO. In a Fortune 500 company, the directors are handpicked for the value and expertise they can bring to assist the company in achieving its goals. As the CEA, your board of directors may include:

- Spouses, parents, and siblings
- Trusted friends
- Professors

- Team owners
- University presidents
- Faith leaders

The board, again, is outside of the corporate hierarchy. You will not necessarily have a "formal board" in your company. But you will have advisors who you can trust to seek advice and counsel. These people may be outside of your general counsel, agent, or PR person, etc. They can be a pastor that you trust dearly, or a brother, uncle, or parent. I am an attorney, but I also have people I refer to as my board members. Some are longtime friends, others are professional acquaintances, but they are all people whose input I trust when I need someone to bounce ideas off of. I know we sometimes hear horror stories about athletes trusting their families and friends. Well, sometimes life-long family and friends are the best advisors and some-times they are not to be trusted! Again, the CEA as leader has to decide on who to trust!

Take Grant Hill, for instance. Grant's mother was a lawyer whose roommate in law school was Hillary Clinton. Grant's father was a professional football player and did extremely well post-football. So, in Grant's case, he had parents that he could trust and rely on for business advice and wise counsel. Those who you trust to influence your decisions should be on your board. Who would you consider putting on your company board of directors?

SHAREHOLDERS

Then you, like a Fortune 500 Company, have your shareholders! These are the individuals and companies that benefit from your earnings and achievements. So, if you go out and create a great brand, image, and likeness; if you perform well on the field or the court; if you create other opportunities off the court, or if you create wealth and even generational wealth . . . your shareholders will benefit. The more money that Microsoft makes, the more its shareholders earn. Your shareholders—in this instance, your closest family members (spouse, kids, parents, siblings)—are looking to you. You are sacrificing your time being away from your family, working to increase the wealth of your family so that they all benefit. When you consider yourself, your family, or others as your shareholders, you will begin to approach your career from a business perspective. They are investing in you when you are away from the home, and they benefit from your company's successes. The other stakeholders are the team(s), universities, and corporate partners with whom you are associated (sportswear, sports drink, auto, etc.) The stakeholders also benefit from your performance and business decisions. When you do well, the stakeholders are enamored with the relationship they share with you. Now you should be able to develop a draft of your organizational chart (including your personal board of directors). See the blank chart in the appendix. In the blank chart you can add names to each position above the position title.

NON-PROFIT ORGANIZATION

A non-profit organization (a charity, foundation, etc.) is another piece that plays a role in your branding. If you are well-liked and have a great image, you will likely gain better corporate partners and sponsors for your tournaments, back-to-school giveaways, or other charitable events you develop or participate in throughout your various communities. Believe it or not, this parallels with the big companies. Nike has Nike Incorporated, but Nike also has a foundation. Chase Bank has a foundation, as do Walmart, Exxon Mobil, United Parcel Service (UPS), and Allstate. Your for-profit entity is a separate entity from your non-profit entity. It is important to understand how the two work together for you. Your for-profit entity is you (your company) and your earnings on and off the field; your non-profit entity is the entity you use to support the causes you believe in and to develop charitable programming. Your non-profit will need an actual board of directors and staff personnel that assist you with your charity and community service projects. Oftentimes, many of your professional representatives (attorney, agent, CPA, etc.), along with one or two of your shareholders, will serve on your non-profit board. In some instances, members of the community you are serving will volunteer their time and resources to assist you.

Of course, many of these concepts and required decisions will be unchartered territory for you. This is where a mentor and/or your personal board of directors can be of the most assistance. Let us revisit Junior Bridgeman for more clarity on this subject.

While he was a player for the University of Louisville, Junior Bridgeman already had his sights on what was next for him after sports. He reached out to John Y. Brown, who would later become the governor of Kentucky, about his experience in purchasing the Kentucky Fried Chicken (KFC) franchise. Brown had purchased the franchise from its founder, Harland Sanders, in 1964, turning it into a multimillion-dollar restaurant business. He sold it in 1971 and reinvested the profits in numerous other ventures, including the American Basketball Association's Kentucky Colonels and the NBA's Boston Celtics and Buffalo Braves. Brown was one of Junior Bridgeman's first mentors. Although this particular mentor had a wealth of knowledge and experience, Junior did not limit himself to one resource alone. He stayed hungry—even when he started playing for the NBA in 1975. In several interviews, he mentions that he went into the league already thinking about what he would do once he retired from the sport. During the first four years of his NBA career, he took law classes at the University of Wisconsin. This decision was likely inspired by John Y. Brown, who briefly practiced law before purchasing the KFC franchise. Although Junior did not complete law school, his mind never veered from what he wanted to do next. In a 2017 interview with *Kentucky to the World*,[3] Junior shared more of his early motivations:

> *I thought that I might get a job working for a Fortune 500 company in some department, because that's what you're conditioned to do. It wasn't until my time representing the players association and collective bargaining that I really got interested in the business world. . . . During the collective bargaining sessions, we'd take a break. We'd be arguing about **per diem** and number of games played and how we travel. To us, that was the most important thing in the world: the game of basketball. But I would watch the owners during the break. They would kind of go to different sides of the room. So I kind of eased my way over there to hear what they were talking about, and they're not talking about basketball. They're talking about business opportunities. . . . What I noticed is how excited they were about this. It was almost like being at the collective bargaining table was a burden for them. They'd rather talk about business opportunities*

---

[3] Evan, Episode 14: "The lessons for us all in Junior Bridgeman's career transformation: NBA star to restaurant mogul," Taped in front of a live audience. Podcast audio, August 8, 2016 @ 9:47 PM. https://rothbrothers.podbean.com/

and the world of business. I said, maybe I'm missing something here . . .

Junior became a mentee of several other NBA team owners, as well as the student of Wendy's franchise owners (from whom he also gained employment to further learn the business model of the company). As mentioned in the previous chapter, Junior's focus and drive paid off, as he is now dubbed one of the wealthiest former NBA players of all time.

A few key points here:

1. You do not need to have the biggest contract to extend your wealth and legacy.

2. You need a post-career plan.

3. You can benefit from mentorship.

You can accomplish your goals with ambition, focus, strategy, and a dream team of professionals advising your organization.

4

The Business Life Cycle
of an Athlete

*"Longevity in this business is about being able to reinvent
yourself or invent the future."*

—Satya Nadella, CEO of Microsoft

"We come into the league, specifically the NFL, at twenty-one, twenty-two years old, and we have to think about retirement at around thirty, whereas the rest of the workforce thinks about retiring around fifty-five, sixty years old." Sterling Sharpe, a former first round pick in the NFL, shared this sage wisdom with me about twenty years ago as we prepared to tee off on a par 3 hole in Katy, TX, and it stuck with me. I will never forget it. Early retirement thinking is totally outside of the norm. Most likely, athletes' parents or professors have no experience in that reality. It is completely different from how the rest of society approaches life and the life cycle of earning.

You have to rethink the idea of the life cycle of earning, because the earning life cycle is much faster for the athlete than it is for the average person or a regular business. You are making X amount of money, which is far more than the typical entrepreneur earns, but the average life cycle of your business as an athlete is about five years for basketball and about half of that for football. So, you have to start thinking about life after sports early, and the earlier you begin to do so, the better-off you will be. By viewing yourself as a CEA now, you are already shifting your mindset from a personal perspective into a business perspective and thus positioning yourself to better prepare for what is next.

Take first-round draft pick, two-time Pro Bowler, and ten-year veteran Mark Fields, for instance. Mark was at the apex of his career when he was diagnosed with Hodgkin's lymphoma (cancer of the lymphatic system). Mark's thumb injury had been taking longer than normal to heal, and upon a doctor's visit and a battery of tests, Mark was given the diagnosis that would change his life forever. Mark was forced to sit out a season and undergo strenuous treatments, hospital stays, and rehabilitation. Remarkably, Mark returned to play after sitting out a year, earning a spot in the Pro Bowl and winning the ESPY Award for NFL Comeback Player of the Year. However, during his post-season diagnosis, Mark's cancer returned and he was forced to retire from the NFL. Despite Mark's inability to play professional football and the costs associated with his healthcare, Mark's lifestyle was not impacted. Mark had adopted the CEA mantra early on in his career and had positioned himself financially to maintain his preferred quality of life. Mark has been in remission for many years to date, and he maintains his pre-retirement lifestyle and continues to build his portfolio of businesses. Mark continues to enjoy a high-quality lifestyle nearly eighteen years after playing his last down of football.

Consider my friend All-Pro NFL Player Sterling Sharpe, whose career was cut short after seven seasons due to a neck injury. Sterling, the older brother of NFL Hall of Famer and co-host of the sports talk show *Undisputed* Shannon Sharpe, was putting together a career worthy of the hall of fame when he injured his neck while blocking during an NFL game. After several medical consultations, Sterling was advised that additional contact to his neck could be fatal or cause paralysis. Sterling underwent extensive surgery and his NFL career came to an abrupt halt. Sterling, like Mark Fields, had adopted the CEA mantra early in his career and had positioned himself for life after the league. Post-NFL, Sterling spent several years as a football analyst/commentator on a few different networks while also managing his various business interests. Sterling can now usually be found on a golf course or at a celebrity golf event. Mark Fields and Sterling Sharpe are the perfect examples of the importance of preparing early for the inevitable end of a playing career, and in each of their cases, a career that ended abruptly due to injury or illness. Planning is key! Taking hold of your career as a

Chief Executive Athlete will position you to be prepared for a high-quality life after your time on the field or court has ended.

The business life cycle of earning typically consists of five stages: thinking, launching, growing, reinventing, and then exiting. The cycle works not only for the entrepreneur but for the athlete who evolves into an entrepreneur by thinking as a CEA.

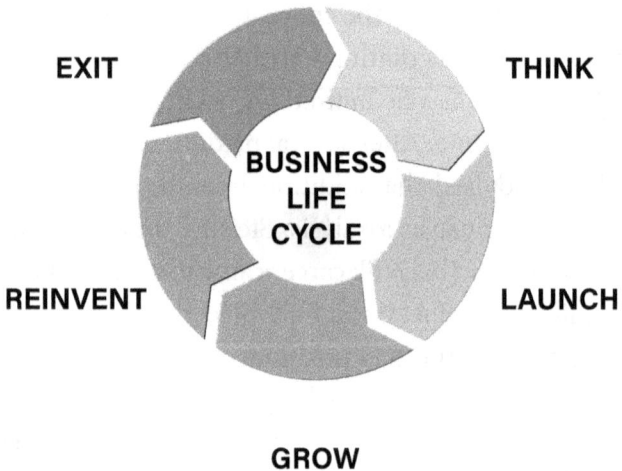

THINK
The thinking stage for the entrepreneur is the daydreaming and the drafting. It is when the individual imagines the type or kind of business he/she wants to create or take part in. Where should it be located? What is the market

for it? How can that market be reached? What products and/or services should be provided for the market? Who is the competition? Are you building the business from scratch, or are you taking over a business that already exists? What resources are needed to launch the business? Are you an investor or active operator? The thinking stage is when the business plan is created.

The thinking stage for an athlete begins long before he gets to the professional level. An athlete must consider how he/she is going to get to the professional rank and then commit to getting there. Many times, that means attending college, making the grades to be eligible, practicing, training, and performing when called upon. To become a professional—and have staying power once one becomes a professional—requires sacrifice (time away from family and friends), discipline (training schedules, diet), and perseverance (injury rehabilitation, support systems, coaches, etc.). Once an athlete reaches his/her goal as a professional athlete, it is imperative to begin imagining what a post-athletic career will look like. The athlete has to envision himself/herself in a different space—not in ten years or five years or even two, but actually next year. Will the athlete pursue a different professional career as an:

- Attorney
- Accountant
- Doctor

- Educator
- Coach
- Member of the military

Or will the athlete pursue business interests, a career as a sport commentator, or passive investments? As a CEA, you must be thinking about your next move and your move if your current revenue stream (based on your performance) is taken away. What will the company (you) do to earn income? The thinking stage for the CEA is ongoing, but it must be addressed sooner rather than later.

LAUNCH

In the business life cycle, the launch is the big day, the big moment. It is a memorable time. You have gone from thinking about a plan to actualizing the plan. You have released your products and/or services to the market. Sales are most likely pretty slow at this point, but fingers crossed, they are steady or even increasing. Marketing is in full effect, but the losses are pretty high. This is the sink-or-swim stage of the business, as the losses will likely outweigh the gains. A strong thinking stage and a strong market paired with a great product and service best positions you for success in the launch stage. Even here, there is still plenty of planning involved—perhaps even more than in the thinking stage.

Athletes in the launch phase are experiencing the reality of their vision. The CEA is profiting from his performance and potentially his image and likeness. It is now imperative that the CEA manage his entity and drive his team to accomplish the goals he set forth in the thinking phase. Now it is time to launch "Prime Time" or "Lil Penny" or any other persona, product, or income-producing idea.

GROW

In the growth stage, you have passed the break-even point. You are generating consistent profits and your list of new customers is continuously rising. It is the moment you have been waiting for. There are several new challenges at this stage, including but not limited to: figuring out how to manage the increased revenue, attending to stakeholders' needs and concerns, staying ahead of the competition, accommodating an expanding staff, etc. In this stage, you might find yourself quoting the timeless passage, "To whom much is given, much is required."

During the growth stage of the CEA, the CEA is managing the success he/she is having, managing expectations, and minimizing mistakes and miscues. Many times, this is the stage when the CEA has to navigate the most "minefields" in the form of lawsuits, character attacks, and attacks on the primary income-producing source, (i.e., your performance on the field/court/sideline). It is critical at this stage that the CEA remains committed to their initial goals and visions, remains level-headed, and acts like a chief executive. The CEA must make the critical decisions that will determine whether the enterprise will continue to succeed or start to erode due to a lapse in judgment, arrogance, or failure to remain involved and engaged.

REINVENT

Inevitably, the business will mature and sales will begin to fluctuate. It is like the human body growing older; you cannot avoid it. Profit margins begin to thin and cash flow stagnates. However, businesses that are not ready to close the doors yet will extend their life cycle by reinventing themselves, investing in new technologies, and studying budding markets. This allows the business to reposition itself in the ever-changing industry and hit the refresh button on its ability to remain relevant and experience additional growth.

Take Coca-Cola for instance: in realizing they needed to begin targeting millennials, they first studied that market. According to Joe Tripodi, the chief marketing and commercial officer, millennials "expect unlimited choice, personalized and delivered through multiple channels at maximum speed." The company listed the values and beliefs of the new generation and figured out a way to align itself with those values. One of the changes it made was its packaging. You might remember the craze of trying to find a Coca-Cola can or bottle with your first name on it.

That was part of the company's reinvention. Another strategy was the Freestyle machine, which is available today in many fast-food restaurants. You grab a cup and choose which flavored soft drink or juice you want. Yet another reinvention of Coca-Cola was joining the health-conscious conversation and partnering with organizations whose primary messaging and focus is health.[4]

Ahh, the reinvent stage for the CEA. It is an ever-critical and treacherous stage. Why, you ask? Well, here is where the CEA is starting to age out of his/her profession; their skills may decline, their performance salary may start to decrease, trends start to shift away from the CEA's skillset, and injuries are career-ending or too hard to overcome. Many athletes who have not used the thinking stage or launch stage struggle to decide what they should do next. It is at this time that many athletes make impulsive decisions that are costly—sometimes too costly to recover from. For instance, once you receive your last paycheck from your respective team or university, your *only* sources of income are your outside business ventures, the earnings on your investment accounts, any remaining payments from past teams, and endorsements, if any. However, the "huge" salary payment that you once were accustomed is

---

[4] Avi Dan, "Just How Does Coca-Cola Reinvent Itself in a Changed World?" Forbes (Forbes Magazine, October 28, 2013), https://www.forbes.com/sites/avidan/2013/10/07/just-how-does-coca-cola-reinvent-itself-in-a-changed-world/#-4c0a34d1a6bb

no longer making its way to your bank account. Hence, if you have not prepared for that moment, that last season, that last paycheck, you are living on your savings. Thus, this stage can be so costly. This is why *preparing* in the thinking stage and *implementing* during the launch stage are so critical. As a reminder, the CEA must prepare for what is next *immediately* upon reaching the collegiate status. More on that in a moment!

To be clear, as a professional athlete, you will have opportunities that are not afforded to others. This includes endorsement opportunities where other companies will pay you and your company to help elevate their brand through your image and likeness (e.g., card signings, product endorsements, appearances, speaking engagements, etc.). Your status or title as a professional athlete or former professional athlete will get you in rooms others do not have access to. Your status will afford you unique opportunities to participate in business opportunities, franchise opportunities, real estate opportunities, auto dealership opportunities, early-stage investments, etc. It will depend on what your particular interests are, but there will be opportunities in business and marketing— even creating your own product and services. Your goal is to take advantage of the many opportunities you, as CEA, are afforded.

EXIT

You do not have to be forced to close the doors. You can and should be very intentional about your exit strategy. Do you want the business to outlive you? Do you want to sell it or hire/promote your successor? If you do plan to sell it, do you know how much the business will be worth? Effective planning will help you make the most of your transition and help you to ensure that you understand the true value of the business and brand that you have taken years to cultivate. Now you are free to retire without worrying about if your savings are enough to last and you can move on to whatever endeavor you envisioned next for your life.

Some players with whom I have worked are extremely talented artists in some capacity and want to develop their art. They may be musicians and want to develop their music or filmmaking skills. They all have varied interests. While sports are providing immediate income, they use that money to fund other interests that have the potential to generate even more income. There are many examples of athletes who have successfully transitioned into the film and television industry. Dwayne Johnson might be one of the most well-known, but there are also Jim Brown, Burt Reynolds, Carl Weathers, Bob Golic, John Amos, and Terry Crews. LeBron James founded a production company, SpringHill Entertainment, through which he has produced numerous films and television shows. Athletes have also turned to music and other arts, so do not overlook your artistic hobbies. They could very well be your *what's next*.

For a CEA who works through the various stages of the business cycle, there are many options for exiting. The CEA that positions himself for the Think, Launch, and Reinvent stages likely has either a wealth of liquid assets (cash, stocks, bonds) or passive income (real estate rents, notes, interest in businesses or equity funds) or various active business(es). Therefore, the CEA with these circumstances has positioned himself/herself to exit on his/her terms. There is no rush or requirement to exit other than lifestyle or preference. The CEA that has failed to prepare himself/herself for the Exit stage will be forced to "exit stage left" with nothing more than memories. This is what we are trying to avoid!

Retire and Redirect

*"I haven't had the time to say, 'I'm retiring.'
But baseball says, 'You're retired.'"*

—Rickey Henderson, retired MLB baseball player, ranked
second in steals in MLB history

Will you know exactly what you want to do when you retire? Most likely, you will not. If you already know what is next, then that is even better. You are already on the right path. If you do not know what is next, then it is not too late. Your team will help you get there. If you put together a formidable team—if you have a good CPA, a good lawyer, a solid agent, and public relations—your team can assist you in determining your post-career goals and the steps required to fulfill those goals.

Just because business ownership and management are discussed in detail in this book does not mean they are the only paths to a successful and comfortable post-playing life. Please understand that. There are varying degrees of risk-takers in the world of money-making. When Warren Buffet purchased more than a billion dollars' worth of

Coca-Cola stock in 1988, his team thought he had lost his mind. Fortunately for Buffet and his team, however, the aggressive investment was worth it, as its return made him one of the richest men in the world.

Then you have moderately aggressive risk-takers. They are also high risk-takers but more calculated and less impulsive than the aggressive risk-taker. The moderately aggressive risk-taker is your average entrepreneur. Ordering ten thousand copies of your book before you have sold even one copy is an example of moderate risk-taking. You understand that business requires some upfront investment before you can profit, and you are willing to take that risk.

Then you have conservative risk-takers: moderately conservative and plain conservative. The moderately conservative risk-taker is willing to take a loss but very little. They desire greater liquidity, meaning if you need to sell an asset for whatever reason, you want to be able to do so quickly and without affecting its market price as much as possible. Then you have the conservative risk-taker, who may say, "I'm just going to take the fifteen million I made, put that in municipal bonds, earn 6 percent a year; and I'm going to collect and live off of my annual interest."

You may not have that risky edge about you. You may not want to go and invest money and take on all the associated risks. Or you may be young and live by the mantra that "scared money don't make money" and you want to "go hard or go home." In the latter case, you will need a team to assist you in your research, help you launch, and give you that necessary framework for operating a successful enterprise.

So, every CEA and every situation is going to be a little different. No matter who you are, what your earnings are, or what your goals are, a team of qualified people can help you get there faster than trying to do it on your own. The "dream team," you will notice, is a recurring theme and subject in this book because it is just that important to your success.

CHAPTER
6

Protect Your Ass(ets)

"Protection of human life can be costly, but so is the neglect of that protection."

—Max Anders, Christian author

Asset protection starts in the Launch stage, when you have begun profiting from your performance and most likely your image and likeness as well. Your conduct and branding both add to your asset protection. From a legal and business perspective, understanding how to conduct business—creating entities to do business versus doing business in your individual name—is a step that needs to be taken to protect your assets. Understanding what type of entity is best suited for your business is also important. Your team, specifically your general counsel and CPA, should help you when it comes to making these decisions.

There are many, many ways to protect your assets. These are the basic concepts to get you started on the right path to proper coverage. In this chapter, we will discuss business entities, prenuptial agreements, trusts, wills, and various types of insurance. While the thought of entities, legal structures, and insurance instruments can seem excessive, especially in the beginning, I cannot stress enough how important each are. It is better to *be* ready than to have to try to get ready at the last minute. Furthermore, you never want to find yourself in the position of losing so much (or all) of what you have worked so hard to earn. I can tell you so many stories of those who skipped this step in fear of costs to realize later the cost of not doing this step correctly is much more costly.

BUSINESS ENTITIES

When starting or expanding a business, you want to think about which legal structure is most appropriate for you and your business. Each entity has its own advantages, disadvantages, and risks. Because they can be state-specific, I will just cover the general information regarding each one here; but be sure to do your own research and include your team before making a decision. Each legal structure has its own tax implications, so again, it is critical to include the appropriate people from your team when considering a legal structure for your business. Here are the most common forms of legal business structures:

Sole Proprietorship: an unincorporated business owned by one owner or a married couple.

Sole proprietorships are the easiest entities to start, maintain, and file taxes for. As the sole owner, however, you are *personally* responsible for your business's debts and liabilities. That means that if someone sues your business, all of your business assets (e.g., real estate, equipment, cash, etc.) and personal assets (e.g., home, vehicles, stocks, cash, etc.) are at risk. You have absolutely no protection against lawsuits. You personally bear all the responsibility and liability for everything that happens in your business.

Example: Everyone brags about how good Betty's cookies are. Betty decides to start selling them. She was advised to get a business license from her county so that she can open a business account with the bank and be able to sell her cookies at local events as well. Betty is a sole proprietor.

General Partnership: two or more people who contribute cash, property, labor, or knowledge to a shared business and also share in that business's gains and losses.

General partnerships are like sole proprietorships, but they are operated by two or more people (who are not married to each other).

Example: Betty's cookie business is booming. Her sister, who is also a great baker, joins her. They decide to name the business: Betty and Suzy's Cookies. They signed an agreement stating how they will split the expenses and profits. Betty and Suzy are now in a legal business partnership.

Limited Partnership: a registered business, as opposed to an unincorporated business, with both active and limited partners (investors and silent partners).

The difference between your business being unincorporated and incorporated is the separation between you and your business. When incorporated, you are essentially giving your business a life of its own. Your business's income is taxed separately from your personal income, and in the event that your business ever has to go to court, your business's name is on the docket, not yours. Limited partners have less liability than active partners and can leave the partnership without dissolving the business partnership. Active partners, also known as general partners, are responsible for all debts and liabilities.

Example: Betty and Suzy would like their cookies to be sold in Target. This would require warehousing, better packaging, more employees, and more financial resources than they have between them. So, they seek out an investor. The investor chooses to invest as a limited partner, and the three now have a limited partnership, with Betty and Suzy acting as the general partner. Here, the general partner is responsible for running the day-to-day operations of the business. The limited partner is only a financial partner and is not involved in the operations of the business. The limited partner is primarily monitoring the financials and anticipating a return on investment. In this scenario, if someone gets sick from a cookie and files a lawsuit against the company, the limited partner is not really affected. The general partner(s) will have to answer and address the concerns of the lawsuit. Limited partners always have the risk of losing their investment, but their personal assets—and their reputation—are not on the line.

Limited Liability Company: a blend of a sole proprietorship, a partnership, and a corporation to ensure that the business's owners (known as members in this case) are not personally responsible for the business's debts or liabilities.

Limited Liability Companies (LLCs) are like sole proprietorships and general partnerships but with the limited liability protections that corporations enjoy. Another advantage is that you can choose how you would like the IRS to tax you as a corporation or as a pass-through entity. According to the IRS, "Most states do not restrict ownership, so members may include individuals, corporations, other LLCs and foreign entities. There is no maximum number of members. Most states also permit 'single-member' LLCs, those having only one owner."[5]

Example: After the scare of potentially being sued, Betty and Suzy learn that it is time to make their business its own separate entity. Had any previous lawsuit prevailed, they could have lost the business and money in their personal bank accounts. If the damages exceeded what they could afford from their business and personal

---

[5] "Limited Liability Company (LLC)," Internal Revenue Service (United States Government), accessed November 16, 2021, https://www.irs.gov/businesses/small-businesses-self-employed/limited-liability-company-llc

bank accounts, then they would have stood to lose their nonexempt personal assets or even had to file for bankruptcy. With an LLC, their personal assets are safe and secure. The same principle applies in reverse as well. If their personal debt is out of hand, creditors cannot touch their business assets. By choosing an LLC as the legal structure to operate their business, Betty and Suzy have now created a legal distinction between their personal and business finances and assets.

Corporation: a legal business entity that is separate from its owner(s) and distributes profits to its shareholders.

Corporations are considered incorporated and have access to many of the same rights and responsibilities as people do. They can enter contracts, loan and borrow money or other assets, sue (and be sued), hire a staff, own assets, and pay taxes. This is why corporations are often referred to as a "legal person." There are two types of corporations: a standard corporation and an "S" corporation.

A standard corporation, also known as a "C" corporation, consists of shareholders, a board of directors, and officers. As an independent legal entity, it exists separately from you or any of its individual shareholders. This is likely the biggest benefit. Compared to the sole proprietor and partnership, standard corporations have far more regulations and tax laws to obey. They also, however, qualify for more tax deductions than any other business entity. The

"C" corporation files its own tax return as its own entity and is totally separate from the individual shareholder(s).

S corporations have the same limited liability as standard corporations, so you do not have to worry about personal liability for debts. The primary difference between the two involves the IRS. With S corporations, your profits and/or losses pass through to your personal tax returns. The IRS taxes them similar to that of a sole proprietorship and general partnership.

Example: Business is booming for Betty and Suzy. Unfortunately, they are also being taxed more. As the income from their LLC increases, so does their self-employment tax. The more they earn, the more they pay. Switching to a corporation lessens their tax burden and increases their retirement contribution options. They now also have to pay themselves as employees, with taxes being deducted from their paychecks just like their employees. Once a corporation, they are both employees and shareholders. All investors become shareholders as well based on the percentage/equity they agreed to. In this example, Betty and Suzy maintain 60 percent ownership and the remaining 40 percent is split among the other shareholders.

Key: The business entity you choose—with the assistance of your team—should provide maximum protection of your assets while decreasing your tax liabilities as much as legally possible. Research your state and discuss with your team to determine what options are available, as each entity carries its own set of pros and cons.

Your business entity is your business's platform, so be sure to discuss your needs and ideas with your legal and financial team to determine which entity will best help you achieve your goals. Establish a solid foundation the first go-round so that you can avoid unwarranted liabilities as you expand and ultimately accomplish the goals you set for yourself.

PRENUPTIAL AGREEMENTS

Prenup is short for prenuptial and it is an agreement between future spouses to make decisions in advance about the assets acquired before and during the marriage and in the event of a divorce. In some states, if no prenup is agreed upon, the money that one spouse earns during the marriage is considered marital property that belongs to both spouses. With a prenup, future spouses can agree that a spouse's income will remain that spouse's separate property if the marriage ends.

Discussing a prenuptial agreement can be a difficult conversation to initiate. Being able to have that discussion, understanding what a prenup does, and getting a qualified professional to help draft the proper documents is in the best interest of you and your spouse.

Sometimes CEAs marry spouses who have assets as well. So, it is not always the athletes, per se. It can be either way or both. Tom Brady and his wife, Gisele Caroline Bündchen, are an excellent example of this. Her net worth is believed to be equal to or greater than his. So, the protection goes both ways. Even if you are single right now, it still helps to know what you want to do when you get to the point of marriage.

Your lawyers will assist you in creating a thorough and concise agreement that defines you and your loved one's unique financial situation in the event of a divorce or even death. Marriage is one of the most sacred and exciting experiences there is, but it is always safe to plan and protect yourself.

TRUSTS

According to Bankrate, a trust is "a legal vehicle that allows a third party, a trustee, to hold and direct assets in a trust fund on behalf of a beneficiary. A trust greatly expands your options when it comes to managing your assets, whether you are trying to shield your wealth from taxes or pass it on to your children."[6] You can fund a trust with assets such as real estate, investments, life insurance, business interests, cash accounts, jewelry, heirlooms, and antiques, etc.

---

[6] James Royal, "What is a Trust?" Investing (Bankrate, LLC., July 9, 2021), https://www.bankrate.com/investing/what-is-a-trust/

It all comes down to understanding how to protect what you have already earned and are earning and protecting you and your family going forward. The trust is a great tool for asset protection. A trust can also protect you and your heirs from creditors under various scenarios—really too many to discuss in the space we have here, but be sure to discuss trusts with your general counsel to understand the types of trusts that extend you protection against creditors. One of the bigger benefits of a trust is the role it plays in transferring property privately at death. Your attorney will be able to thoroughly assist you in this option as well.

WILLS

Wills provide direction as to who gets your property—your real estate and personal property—upon your death. Personal property is everything that is not real property, also known as real estate. All of your personal property and real property can be placed in a trust, and this will help avoid many issues associated with the probate process.

The probate process occurs when someone dies and the lawyer takes the will—if there is a will—and presents it to the court. A properly drafted and executed will instructs the court on how all the decedent's (deceased person's) property should be transferred. If there is no will, then there is an entirely separate set of property transfer rules that are governed differently in each state. The probate process is a public process, meaning that the will and the decedent's assets are made available via public filing. However, if everything is in a trust, then it passes through the trustee and you do not have to rely on the probate process for the transfer of the majority (if not all) of the decedent's assets. A trust provides privacy, so the public will not know how much your heirs are receiving.

The two main types of wills are living wills and last wills. A living will is a written statement that details what you want to happen if you become mentally (and sometimes also physically) incapacitated. It allows you to speak for yourself when you cannot speak for yourself. Everyone should have a living will. You should prioritize creating one in the event that you are diagnosed with a terminal illness, have an unexpected accident rendering you incapacitated, or have an upcoming surgery. Without one, your closest family members are forced to make these decisions on your behalf and that can cause unnecessary stress, regret, and even family tensions.

A last will and testament is the most common type of will. It is the one we hear about the most, and it instructs the court on the transfer of property upon your death. Your last will should also name an executor of your choice. This person is also sometimes called a personal representative. They are responsible for settling your final affairs and guiding your estate through the probate process. The probate process is required to transfer ownership of your assets to the proper beneficiaries (even if they are charities). As previously mentioned, the absence of a will will not avoid this process; the biggest difference is, the transfer will not be based on your wishes but rather the laws of the state in which you reside (for some examples, google articles on the deaths of Prince, James Brown, and NFL star Derrick Thomas).

INSURANCE

Insurance is your most basic form of asset protection for your property and yourself. Insurance provides numerous benefits, including protection for you and your family, less stress during difficult times, increased financial security, better peace of mind, and a legacy to leave behind. In some cases, insurance is required for a particular asset. And in some cases, it is provided for you. Let's take a look at a few different types of insurance.

Disability

Disability insurance is especially useful for CEAs who play the more aggressive sports like football or hockey, and especially if your entire contract value is not guaranteed. An athlete participating in any sport at the college level should get a disability policy, especially if you are projected to be drafted to one of the professional leagues. For some highly rated players, the disability policies are paid for by the schools and/or conferences.

There are disability policies in place to protect two things: 1) In the event that the player cannot ever play again, he/she will collect some form of financial benefit. 2) If the player was projected for the 1st round and then drops to the fourth or sixth round because of an injury suffered midseason during collegiate play, then there is a rider that will make up the difference in what would have been earned versus what was actually received in terms of compensation based on the draft position.

Health Insurance
Health insurance helps protect you from expensive (and sometimes unexpected) medical costs.

If you are on a team, playing or coaching, then you will have access to health insurance. The critical piece here is understanding how to remain insured when you are no longer employed. It is important to review your league's Collective Bargaining Agreement (CBA) to better understand the availability of post-employment health insurance benefits for you and your family.

Life Insurance
It is essential to have adequate life insurance to cover you in the event of an untimely death. The benefits will provide a great financial value to your family. This is particularly important for young athletes with spouses and children. Life insurance will ensure that your family receives the equivalent or similar income you were projected to receive

during your earning years. The insurance proceeds help your family maintain the lifestyle you would have provided if not for your untimely death.

General Liability

General liability insurance just covers your business—protecting the basic equipment, cars, office, etc. No matter what type of business you have—real estate, flipping cars, a barbershop—you need to have a basic business policy. It protects you and shields your personal assets. If you are buying property, you need to have insurance. If you buy houses to rent out for passive income, you need insurance on each house, but you also need insurance on the company that you are buying the houses through. Here, say you form a limited liability company (LLC) called Ball Player's LLC to purchase rental properties—then you will need an insurance policy on this entity and separate insurance on each property you purchase. The insurance provides additional asset protection for your company(ies), and for you and your individual assets.

Errors and Omissions

You may need professional liability insurance depending on what you are doing. There are some CEAs now doing venture capital fundraising and digital marketing. So, errors and omissions insurance (E&O) and professional liability insurance protects them in the event that something goes wrong, especially in the area of raising funds. It could be an issue of mistake, misrepresentation, or theft, and E&O protects your personal assets from your business liabilities.

Keyman Life

Keyman life insurance is a bit technical. You may or may not ever need it. However, it is a basic insurance used when two or more people are in a business and both are "rainmakers" for the business, i.e., they both bring value to the company. In Keyman life insurance, the business can take out insurance on each one of them. This way, if one or the other dies, for instance, then the business will receive money that essentially replaces the income of the deceased person. This policy helps the business stay afloat rather than lose what that person would have contributed. It can also be of good use for the surviving business owner to use the funds to provide a financial benefit to the deceased owner's family.

These are all various options for wealth preservation and tools to protect your assets. When considering your goals, it is best to visit with your team to get a better understanding of which financial and legal tools are in your best interest.

Coaches

"Selecting the right person for the right job is the largest part of coaching."

—Phil Crosby, American business executive (one of the first American executives to focus on the measurement of quality)

Players and coaches are equally critical to a team's success. Coaching is probably one of the most rewarding and demanding jobs one can have. Practice to practice, game to game, season to season, coaches have the unique opportunity to develop players on and off the field. Players who have not played on a team in more than 40 years still recall the life lessons they learned from a coach. That is the kind of impact coaches have on the lives of their players.

As a coach, you study and work on your players as individuals while simultaneously setting goals for the entire team and helping to build a plan to accomplish those team goals. As you know, it is more than just coordinating practices and managing game day. It is more than just the sport itself. You take on a role as a mentor and sometimes as a parental figure. The mental aspect of your role is often overlooked and undervalued, especially in the professional league, where, with the flip of a "switch," your whole world can change.

Head coaches in the NFL have an exceptionally high turnover rate. If the wins are not adding up fast enough and the fans start losing hope, desperate team owners often see getting rid of the coach as the quickest way to restore hope in the fanbase. New England Patriots head coach Bill Belichick once noted that all coaches in the NFL are on a one-year contract. That is a lot of expectation and pressure packed into one season!

There is a little more breathing room with the NCAA, but that has its own set of disadvantages as well (primarily a longer list of people to answer to, including alumni). This is not to say that one is better than the other. Not at all! It is only to emphasize that it is critical to—along with the players—see yourself as a business and position yourself accordingly. *The day you are hired is the first day you are closer to being fired!* It is in your best interest to think that way. Three or five years in, you should still be thinking about what is next. Retiring? Transitioning? There are coaches who have done extremely well on the court or field but then have had something perceived as negative happen in their personal lives and now schools do not want to hire them for fear of retribution from the alumni and public alike. Things happen in life and another opportunity may not come, and it could have absolutely nothing to do with one's coaching ability. Some coaches have nine lives, and some have one. That is just how the industry works.

YOUR CONTRACT NEGOTIATIONS
In examining the coach's role as a CEA, let's take a look at contract negotiations first.

Salary
Salary is one of the primary things to consider in your contract negotiation. You have your base annual salary, but then there are other nuances to consider such as compensation for winning the conference and national championships, graduation rates, generating game guarantees, pay and benefits for your staff, and post-termination benefits. So, while you could potentially earn $3 million dollars per year, your base salary may only be a third or fourth of that. The difference in income may be generated from outside the team/professional organization or university system.

When coaching for a public university, you are a state employee, and in many cases, the highest-paid employee in the state. The highest-paid state employee in Texas, for instance, is a football coach. In 2018, Texas A&M handed Jimbo Fisher a ten-year, $75 million contract. The headlines read that he makes $7.5 million dollars per year, but his base salary is $500,000 and there is another $7 million dollars annually in "supplemental income." The contract also includes the "use of two luxury vehicles" and a country club membership. So, your contract includes more than your base salary; it can include a number of things: base salary but also athletic brand endorsements for using their apparel and equipment, naming rights for radio and/or tv shows, podcasts, etc.

Most coaches speak well because they are skilled communicators. Speaking at events. Writing books. Owning a company. There are various opportunities. You have to already be preparing and working toward what you will do next. Sometimes you are paid so much money in a contract that as long as you manage your money effectively, you do not have to worry yourself with the pressure of what is next. Until you get to that point, however, always keep in mind that each day you are moving closer to your termination date.

Your negotiation concerns are a little different than a player's negotiation concerns. Players do not have much leverage because their contract is a standard contract developed by the Players Association for each league. They are only negotiating their compensation and maybe bonus structure. For a coach, however, there is a lot more to negotiate. Do you want private travel for your family? How many tickets to a suite do you want? Do you want a private suite for all athletic events? A car allowance? You name it, and it is probably on the table.

Then there are your off-the-field earnings to be nego-tiated, like apparel deals! Deion Sanders recently signed a coaching contract with Jackson State University (JSU). One of the conditions for signing Sanders, however, meant that JSU would have to switch from Nike to Under Armour, a competing sports apparel company that Sand-ers has endorsed for many years. It was not just a matter of scratching out their name on one piece of paper and signing it on another; JSU had to pay their way out of their Nike contract. That shows the value that Sanders brought to the table, as well as his firmness in negotiation. It is im-perative to negotiate those things that are of importance to you during your initial courting and negotiations.

Several factors are at play when it comes to your com-pensation package: the type of sport (football, basketball, and baseball coaches are the highest earners), the size of the school or athletic department, your geographic loca-tion, your educational background, and your experience.

Also bear in mind, however, that if it is your first time as a head coach, you will likely not make as much as the highest-paid coaches. At the time of writing this, Nick Saban has been head football coach at Alabama for four-teen years. Before that, he was head coach for the Miami Dolphins, Louisiana State University, Michigan State, and the University of Toledo. He has been a head coach since 1989, has won five national championships (three of them in a four-year span), and holds armfuls of "coach of the year" awards. A first- or second-year head coach simply cannot expect to match Saban's $9.1 million in annual compensation.

You can get close, though! Take Dabo Swinney, head coach of Clemson. He got his first head coach position in 2009 and already makes $8.3 million. Peel the layers back, and you will see that he has a master of business administration, various bowl participations as a player, about fifteen years of assistant coaching experience with nine of those years leading to bowl participation, and seventeen bowl seasons as a coach.

Again, it is market-based. Know where you stand in the market. Although you might not be paid as much as someone else, you still want to make sure you are getting adequate pay. That works in the best interest of the organization as well, because if you are underpaid, then you will obviously always be on the lookout for the next job. Your representation should negotiate effectively so you will get what you want in your employment contract.

Bonuses for Conferences and Championships

There is compensation for winning the conference, but you have to negotiate that. If not, you do not get compensated—your team will win the conference and you will not get extra compensation. If you are in certain schools, in certain conferences, some bowls will be more significant. If you are at one of the Big Ten schools, for instance (e.g.,

Michigan State or Ohio State), going to the Rose Bowl is a big deal. That is their Super Bowl!

In 2019, Ohio State's football coach, Ryan Day, was paid $4.5 million annually. He was paid $50,000 for being the East Division champion in the Big Ten and another $100,000 for winning the Big Ten Championship game. For making it to the semifinals, he got another quarter of a million dollars. Had Ohio State won the Fiesta Bowl, he would have earned another $100,000. But let us be clear—these incentives and bonuses are a part of his negotiated contract terms. You cannot expect to be compensated for your accomplishments if you have not previously agreed to such compensation before the triggering events take place.

Your Assistants

You also have to be mindful of your assistants. How much will the university/athletic department budget to pay your staff? There is your staff's base salary, of course, then also your staff/assistants' bonus pool. If you win the conference and you get $25,000, what do your assistants get? That has to be negotiated. As you know, when the head coach accepts another position at another institution or gets fired, everyone below him usually has to leave and/or gets terminated as well. That is quite a bit of pressure on everyone. The head coach has to be mindful of his staff. They are usually following him cross-country to support him as an assistant or office staff member. That requires a lot of trust and faith, so the head coach should consider his staff and the impact of the contract terms on the staff when negotiating.

After You Leave
You need a legal person involved to deal with buyout clauses (some argue these clauses are illegal) and termination clauses. What are the termination-for-cause provisions? Without cause? And what happens then? What if you are offered a position at a different institution or professional organization? How do you get out of your current contract? All of these legal clauses are part of a coach's deal, which is a little different than a player's contract.

There are also your health and insurance benefits to consider—for yourself and your staff. For one coach I represented, I put in his contract that he would receive health benefits for six more months and his staff for two additional months from the termination date. Neither the coach nor the school had ever thought about that! To bring this point home, let us consider the fact that the previous coach and all the staff who had just been terminated had lost all benefits at the time of termination. The head coach agreed to a settlement amount, but the assistants and office staff were only going to receive their last eligible wages and no further health or insurance benefits. In negotiating, my position was that "You cannot expect my client to be successful when his assistants are constantly worried about their wages and the impact of termination. All parties need to be able to breathe if terminated and have fair transition time to their next opportunity."

When to Say No!

Sometimes a team or school will compensate assistant coaches to stay. That is not a bad situation, depending on who you are and what your situation is. Let us say, for instance, that you are at LSU as an offensive coordinator. They are paying you $1 million. You just had a couple of great seasons, including winning the championship in 2019. Now you are being courted to be head coach for a couple of different teams.

If LSU says they will make you the highest-paid offensive coordinator in the country, putting you over $3 million a year, how do you evaluate that offer? I will probably advise the coach to look at his home situation and consider questions like: Am I single or married? Do I have children? If so, how old are they? What are my other opportunities? What other schools are courting me? Are the offers really good jobs, or are they "just" head coaching jobs? Do I want to be a head coach right now? Is this a positive move for my career? Will this offer help me move toward my ultimate goal?

Consider this: You could ruin your career by taking a bad position, even if it is a top position. Consequently, you may never get a head coaching position again. Just taking a head coaching position is not always a positive.

You have to think beyond just being a head coach. The title is not enough. You may be better off staying as an assistant coach for another year or so. Every year is a shakeup!

Also consider the fact that head coaches take all the heat. The buck stops with you! When it comes to wins, losses, and players' conduct, the media, university officials, and professional team representatives do not seek explanations from the assistant coaches. The head coach gets to address those issues.

Trademark It

As with players, coaches have the same concern and responsibility to protect their name and image. Sometimes coaches come up with slogans that they carry with them from place to place. That is an outside income opportunity. It may not immediately convert to cash, but over time, consumers begin gravitating toward the slogan.

Sometimes the public will take something a coach said twenty years ago and realize how brilliant it was. Then it becomes trendy and valuable! You have to protect it along the way, because you do not know where it will lead.

For example, after Clemson beat Notre Dame in October 2015, Dabo Swinney said during a live interview, "I can't give you guts, and I can't give you heart. And tonight, it was BYOG. It was Bring Your Own Guts." Before he walked off the field, it was already a catchphrase that went on to go viral on Twitter, Instagram, Facebook, YouTube, and even ESPN. Less than a week later, his legal team applied to protect those words, BYOG, Bring Your Own Guts, as a registered trademark. Swinney also has trademarks for his names, including "Dabo" and "Dabo Swinney."

In addition to Swinney's base salary of more than $3 million for the season, another $500,000 was added as an annual licensing fee so that the school could legally use his name, image, and likeness. That only happened because he protected himself through registered trademarks. He protected himself that way only because he had a legal team to alert him that it needed to be done.

UTILIZE YOUR DREAM TEAM

The principal point here is having good representation, understanding your market value, and structuring a package that includes adequate salary and outside income. So many people are excited at the opportunities and potential numbers but lose sight of the big picture. You go from making $150,000 as an assistant to being offered $700,000 or $1,000,000.00. It is life-changing money! Having representation and advisors ready to assist you is critical.

You may be surprised that handshake deals still happen. If you are feeling like the little person in the room, desperately wanting the opportunity, you may not request a written contract out of fear that you will offend someone. Your legal team will ensure there is a written contract. There are so many more nuances to a coach's contract than there are to a players. You have to understand the budget before you sign a contract because it impacts what you will be paid, what your assistants will be paid, your recruiting resources, your allotment for travel, etc. Adequate representation and having the right team will help you assess that budget.

Most agents are lawyers, but not all. If you have an agent who is not a lawyer and you are relying on that agent to address contractual clauses and provisions, it is a gamble. You are taking a real chance. If your agent is not an attorney, you should have legal representation on your team. For instance, if you are co-hosting a TV or radio show, are you limited to only doing that TV/radio show for the school or can you venture off and do a national show? Does the car dealership that paid you to use your image have exclusive rights to your image? These are all things that your legal counsel can assist you with.

———————

The goal is not to get ready but to be ready. Know your value on the market, have a plan for your assistants, consider what will happen when you are no longer employed with the team or have another opportunity presented before your current contract ends, protect your assets (including your intellectual property), and most importantly, have a dream team and actually utilize their guidance.

Conclusion

"Always look for the fool in the deal.
If you don't find one, it's you."

—Mark Cuban, governor of the Dallas Mavericks,
technology entrepreneur, philanthropist

Congratulations on being chosen for the opportunity of a lifetime. Whether you are a player or a coach, working for a college or a professional organization, you are in the position to change your life forever. As positions become more equitable, we will begin to see more and more people taking advantage of opportunities that no one in their families or perhaps their entire circles have ever experienced. The goal of this book is to get you thinking proactively about protecting your career, your brand, and yourself.

I have seen it too many times before where players and coaches get caught up in a bad contract, and then they try to make it up or recover in their second contract. I want you to get it right the first time around. You will inevitably still make mistakes and learn lessons from those mistakes, but when it comes to how you are paid, what you are paid, and your additional income streams, the seven chapters in this book were designed to start you off on the right foot.

You are not just a player or a coach. You are the CEA, the top dog, the highest-ranking person on your dream team; you are the one with the last word! You most impact the value of your business. What are your products and services? Why are you attractive to investors? What makes you who you are? What distinguishes you from others? Own it. Perfect it. Brand it. Protect it. And, of course, monetize it.

The best part about this is that you do not have to go at it alone. In fact, you should not. From the time you started, you have been surrounded by mentors. Now it is time to be more intentional about it. That means going through your contacts and reaching out to those who have already been where you are trying to go and who can add input and value to your decision-making process. Some of these people can help you fill in the rest of your dream team. How do you go about finding an agent (or deciding on one)? Or a good attorney? Ask your new and past coaches who they used and what they wish they had known in the early stages of their career regarding their counsel. Your dream team is like your sword and your shield—on and off the court/field.

As I have stated many times in this book, every day that you lace up your shoes to play or coach, you are one day closer to your last day playing or coaching. That insight is not to burden you with more pressure or anxiety. It is to prepare you. It is so that when that final day comes, you will be ready. You will have already been through the Thinking stage and quite possibly the Launching and Growing stages as well. You will have the resources to

Reinvent when the time comes and to Exit comfortably. That is the goal. That is what it means to protect yourself, to not become a victim of an ever-repeating narrative of rich people losing everything. That goes for having wealth and then losing wealth, as well as losing wealth before you ever gain it. Business legal structures, prenuptial agreements, trusts, wills, insurances, and trademarks are valuable tools.

There are so many new and shifting opportunities, including chances for college players to monetize their names and brands. This will be new territory for everyone, so you have to be prepared. You also do not want to let the money distract you. You are paid to play or coach. The opportunities derived from the sport are still based on your performance. Excellent service is paramount to your success. Prioritize your position. Give it your all in every game and every practice, and the likes, follows, and deals with come. You may not have full control over how long your athletic career lasts, but you do have control over how you handle your time and resources during your playing or coaching career. Safeguard your reputation. Steer clear of potential downfalls. Keep your head in the game. And always be on the lookout for the next opportunity.

Everyone's situation is different, so it is impossible to cover every single detail or likely occurrence. However, now that these topics are in mind, you will likely think of more questions to ask. Curiosity is such an undervalued skill. Curiosity is a powerful tool for improving your life. It goes back to the old saying that the more you know, the more you realize what you do not know. If this book made you more curious, that is a good thing. You are more alert; your eyes and ears are open wider. You cannot be fooled as easily. Asking questions serves several purposes, including making you a better leader and more likeable in general. No one cares for a know-it-all.

You might also be thinking of more opportunities to explore, which is another step in the right direction. If you are just taking your check for playing or coaching and going home, then you are shorting yourself. The intent is not to overextend yourself but to find opportunities that align with your goals and lifestyle and can put you in the best position possible. Hopefully you are also thinking about more people to reach out to. Your college coach was not just a coach or teacher, but a possible member of your personal board of directors. The same for that friend of the family who has a wealth of knowledge regarding business, the game, deals, and contracts.

If you are already thinking differently, you are on the right track. Do not make it harder than it has to be. Focus on your career one step at a time. That is how wealth is built and legacies are made. One step at a time. Build your team, consider where you are in the business cycle and what is next, always be mindful of retirement and redirection, and protect your assets like your life depends on it—because it does. You are already one of the chosen few just to be in the position you are in. Now it is time to max-imize—the smart way—as the Chief Executive Athlete.

I am here to help!

Shannon A. Holmes, J.D., M.B.A.

Appendix

CHIEF EXECUTIVE ATHLETE

(C.E.A.)
Organization chart

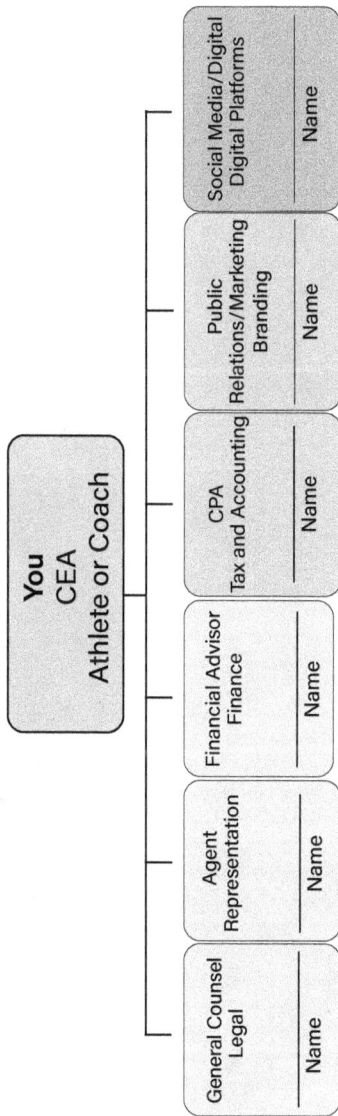

You
CEA
Athlete or Coach

General Counsel Legal	Agent Representation	Financial Advisor Finance	CPA Tax and Accounting	Public Relations/Marketing Branding	Social Media/Digital Digital Platforms
Name	Name	Name	Name	Name	Name

About the Author

Attorney Shannon Anthony Holmes has always enjoyed mentoring, coaching, and representing athletes. Shannon founded his law practice in Dallas, Texas, where he provides legal counsel to professional athletes, licensed professionals, business owners, entertainers, and serial entrepreneurs.

Shannon possesses a bachelor of arts in economics and a master of business administration. He completed his Juris Doctor at Thurgood Marshall School of Law. In his spare time, he is a youth coach and mentor.

Shannon enjoys golf, family, and traveling. He resides in Colleyville, Texas, with his wife, Dr. Jeane' Simmons Holmes, and twins, Bryce and Bailee.

To connect, email him at
shannon@shannonaholmes.com

www.ingramcontent.com/pod-product-compliance
Lightning Source LLC
Chambersburg PA
CBHW071457210326
41597CB00018B/2586